2 **MAKE A SWATC** pattern stitch, choc Make a beginning (or larger swatch using the correct multiple for the beginning chain. Crochet in your selected pattern until you have a square swatch.

3 **MEASURE THE GAUGE.** If you like your pattern stitch swatch, it's time to measure the gauge to determine the number of chains needed to design your project. Lay the swatch, right side up, on a flat, smooth surface. Measure the width of two full repeats of the multiple. Let's say two repeats measure 1". Now do the math.
Example: If two repeats of the multiple measure 1" and there are two chains in one multiple, you know it takes four chains to equal 1".

4 **PLAN THE PROJECT.** Decide what finished measurement you'd like, then figure how many chains are needed for the beginning chain.
Example: Using the 2 + 5 multiple again, let's say you are making a scarf with a finished measurement of 8" wide and your gauge is 2 repeats of the multiple per inch. Multiply 2 (repeats of the multiple) x 2 (stitches in one multiple) for a total of 4 chains. Then multiply 4 (chains) x 8 (width of project) for a total of 32 chains. You would then add 5 chains to equal 37, giving you a multiple of 2 + 5 chains. Work the pattern stitch to the desired length — just be sure to finish the row repeat.

Hint: Do not hesitate to add or subtract chains in order for your beginning chain to correspond with the multiple of your chosen pattern stitch.

Now that you have the basic guidelines for designing, choose a pattern stitch that sparks your imagination. Match it with that yarn you have been itching to use and let the sky be the limit!

PATTERN STITCHES

EXTENDED TR

Multiple of 2 + 1 chs.

Row 1 (Right side)**:** Dc in fourth ch from hook **(3 skipped chs count as first dc)** and in each ch across.

To work Extended Treble Crochet (abbreviated ex tr), YO twice, insert hook in next st, YO and pull up a loop (4 loops on hook), (YO and draw through one loop on hook, YO and draw through 2 loops on hook) 3 times. Push ex tr to **right** side.

Row 2: Ch 1, turn; sc in first sc, (work ex tr, sc in next sc) across.

Row 3: Ch 3 **(counts as first dc)**, turn; dc in next st and in each st across.

Repeat Rows 2 and 3 for pattern.

LONG SC BRICKS

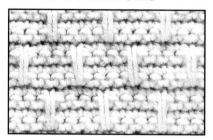

Multiple of 4 chs.

Row 1 (Wrong side)**:** Sc in second ch from hook and in each ch across.

Rows 2-5: Ch 1, turn; sc in each sc across.

To work Long Single Crochet (abbreviated LSC), working **around** previous 3 rows **(Fig. 3, page 32)**, insert hook in sc 3 rows **below** next sc, YO and pull up a loop even with last sc made, YO and draw through both loops on hook.

Row 6: Ch 1, turn; sc in first 3 sc, (work LSC, sc in next 3 sc) across.

Rows 7-9: Ch 1, turn; sc in each sc across.

Row 10: Ch 1, turn; sc in first sc, work LSC, (sc in next 3 sc, work LSC) across to last sc, sc in last sc.

Rows 11-13: Ch 1, turn; sc in each sc across.

Repeat Rows 6-13 for pattern.

SHELLS & LACE

Multiple of 6 + 2 chs.

To work Shell, 5 dc in st indicated.

Row 1 (Right side)**:** Sc in second ch from hook, ★ skip next 2 chs, work Shell in next ch, skip next 2 chs, sc in next ch; repeat from ★ across.

Row 2: Ch 5 **(counts as first dc plus ch 2)**, turn; sc in center dc of next Shell, ch 2, dc in next sc, ★ ch 2, sc in center dc of next Shell, ch 2, dc in next sc; repeat from ★ across.

Row 3: Ch 6 **(counts as first dc plus ch 3)**, turn; sc in next sc, ch 3, dc in next dc, ★ ch 3, sc in next sc, ch 3, dc in next dc; repeat from ★ across.

Row 4: Ch 1, turn; sc in first dc, ★ ch 2, dc in next sc, ch 2, sc in next dc; repeat from ★ across.

Row 5: Ch 1, turn; sc in first sc, (work Shell in next dc, sc in next sc) across.

Repeat Rows 2-5 for pattern.

V-ST PATTERN

Multiple of 3 + 1 chs.

Row 1 (Right side)**:** Dc in fourth ch from hook **(3 skipped chs count as first dc)** and in each ch across.

Row 2: Ch 3 **(counts as first dc, now and throughout)**, turn; dc in next dc and in each dc across.

To work V-St, (dc, ch 1, dc) in dc indicated.

Row 3: Ch 3, turn; skip next dc, work V-St in next dc, (skip next 2 dc, work V-St in next dc) across to last 2 dc, skip next dc, dc in last dc.

Row 4: Ch 3, turn; dc in next dc, 2 dc in next ch-1 sp, (skip next dc, dc in next dc, 2 dc in next ch-1 sp) across to last 2 dc, skip next dc, dc in last dc.

Row 5: Ch 3, turn; dc in next dc and in each dc across.

Repeat Rows 3-5 for pattern.

EYELET BLOCKS

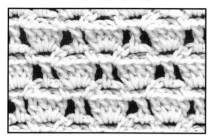

Multiple of 8 + 6 chs.

Row 1 (Wrong side)**:** Sc in second ch from hook, ★ ch 3, skip next 3 chs, sc in next ch; repeat from ★ across.

Row 2: Ch 3 **(counts as first dc)**, turn; 4 dc in first ch-3 sp, ★ ch 1, dc in next ch-3 sp, ch 1, 4 dc in next ch-3 sp; repeat from ★ across, dc in last sc.

Row 3: Ch 1, turn; sc in first dc, ch 3, (sc in next ch-1 sp, ch 3) across to last 5 dc, skip next 4 dc, sc in last dc.

Row 4: Ch 4, turn; dc in first ch-3 sp, ch 1, ★ 4 dc in next ch-3 sp, ch 1, dc in next ch-3 sp, ch 1; repeat from ★ across, dc in last sc.

Row 5: Ch 1, turn; sc in first dc, ch 3, skip first ch-1 sp, (sc in next ch-1 sp, ch 3) across to last dc, skip last dc and next ch, sc in next ch.

Repeat Rows 2-5 for pattern.

SC MAGIC

Multiple of 5 + 3 chs.

Row 1 (Right side)**:** 2 Dc in fifth ch from hook, ch 1, 2 dc in next ch, ★ skip next 3 chs, 2 dc in next ch, ch 1, 2 dc in next ch; repeat from ★ across to last 2 chs, skip next ch, dc in last ch.

Row 2: Ch 3 **(counts as first dc, now and throughout)**, turn; (2 dc, ch 1, 2 dc) in each ch-1 sp across, skip next 2 dc, dc in next ch.

Row 3: Ch 3, turn; (2 dc, ch 1, 2 dc) in next ch-1 sp, ★ ch 2, skip next 2 dc, sc **tightly** around sp of last 2 rows *(Fig. a)*, ch 2, (2 dc, ch 1, 2 dc) in next ch-1 sp; repeat from ★ across to last 3 dc, skip next 2 dc, dc in last dc.

Fig. a

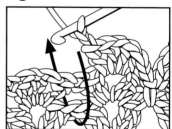

Row 4: Ch 3, turn; (2 dc, ch 1, 2 dc) in next ch-1 sp, ★ skip next 2 ch-2 sps, (2 dc, ch 1, 2 dc) in next ch-1 sp; repeat from ★ across, skip next 2 dc, dc in last dc.

Row 5: Ch 3, turn; (2 dc, ch 1, 2 dc) in each ch-1 sp across, skip next 2 dc, dc in last dc.

Repeat Rows 3-5 for pattern.

PUFF ST BOX

Multiple of 9 + 8 chs.

Row 1 (Right side): Dc in fourth ch from hook **(3 skipped chs count as first dc)**, ch 2, ★ skip next 2 chs, dc in next 7 chs, ch 2; repeat from ★ across to last 4 chs, skip next 2 chs, dc in last 2 chs.

To work Puff St (uses one dc), ★ YO, insert hook in dc indicated, YO and pull up a loop even with last dc made; repeat from ★ 4 times **more**, YO and draw through all 11 loops on hook.

Row 2: Ch 3 **(counts as first dc, now and throughout)**, turn; dc in next dc, ch 2, ★ skip next ch-2 sp and next dc, 2 dc in next dc, ch 1, skip next dc, work Puff St in next dc, ch 1, skip next dc, 2 dc in next dc, ch 2; repeat from ★ across to last ch-2 sp, skip last ch-2 sp, dc in last 2 dc.

Row 3: Ch 3, turn; dc in next dc, ch 2, ★ skip next ch-2 sp, dc in each st and in each ch across to next ch-2 sp, ch 2; repeat from ★ across to last ch-2 sp, skip last ch-2 sp, dc in last 2 dc.

Row 4: Ch 3, turn; dc in next dc, ch 2, ★ dc in next dc, (ch 1, skip next dc, dc in next dc) 3 times, ch 2; repeat from ★ across to last 2 dc, dc in last 2 dc.

Row 5: Ch 3, turn; dc in next dc, ch 2, ★ dc in next dc, (dc in next ch and in next dc) 3 times, ch 2; repeat from ★ across to last 2 dc, dc in last 2 dc.

Repeat Rows 2-5 for pattern.

CLUSTER ROWS

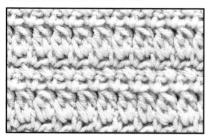

Multiple of 2 chs.

Row 1 (Wrong side)**:** Sc in second ch from hook, ★ ch 1, skip next ch, sc in next ch; repeat from ★ across.

Rows 2 and 3: Ch 1, turn; sc in first sc, (ch 1, sc in next sc) across.

To work Cluster (uses one ch-1 sp), ★ YO, insert hook in sp indicated, YO and pull up a loop, YO and draw through 2 loops on hook; repeat from ★ once **more**, YO and draw through all 3 loops on hook.

Row 4: Ch 4 **(counts as first dc plus ch 1)**, turn; (work Cluster in next ch-1 sp, ch 1) across, dc in last sc.

Row 5: Ch 1, turn; sc in first dc, ch 1, skip next ch-1 sp, (sc in next ch-1 sp, ch 1) across to last ch-1 sp, skip last ch-1 sp, sc in last dc.

Rows 6 and 7: Ch 1, turn; sc in first sc, (ch 1, sc in next sc) across.

Repeat Rows 4-7 for pattern.

SLIP ST TEXTURE

Multiple of 10 + 6 chs.

Row 1 (Right side)**:** Slip st in second ch from hook and in next 4 chs, (hdc in next 5 chs, slip st in next 5 chs) across.

Work in Back Loops Only throughout *(Fig. 1, page 31)*.

Row 2: Turn; slip st in first 5 slip sts, (hdc in next 5 hdc, slip st in next 5 slip sts) across.

Row 3: Ch 2, turn; hdc in first 5 slip sts, (slip st in next 5 hdc, hdc in next 5 slip sts) across.

Row 4: Ch 2, turn; hdc in first 5 hdc, (slip st in next 5 slip sts, hdc in next 5 hdc) across.

Row 5: Turn; slip st in first 5 hdc, (hdc in next 5 slip sts, slip st in next 5 hdc) across.

Repeat Rows 2-5 for pattern.

7

PICOT LACE

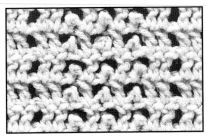

Multiple of 10 + 3 chs.

To work Picot, ch 3, slip st in third ch from hook, ch 1.

Row 1 (Right side)**:** Dc in fourth ch from hook **(3 skipped chs count as first dc)** and in next ch, work Picot, (skip next ch, dc in next ch, work Picot) twice, ★ skip next ch, dc in next 2 chs, ch 1, skip next ch, dc in next 2 chs, work Picot, (skip next ch, dc in next ch, work Picot) twice; repeat from ★ across to last 4 chs, skip next ch, dc in last 3 chs.

Row 2: Ch 3 **(counts as first dc, now and throughout)**, turn; dc in next 2 dc, work Picot, (skip next Picot, dc in next dc, work Picot) twice, ★ skip next Picot, dc in next 2 dc, ch 1, dc in next 2 dc, work Picot, (skip next Picot, dc in next dc, work Picot) twice; repeat from ★ across to last Picot, skip last Picot, dc in last 3 dc.

Repeat Row 2 for pattern.

Last Row: Ch 3, turn; dc in next 2 dc, ch 1, (skip next Picot, dc in next dc, ch 1) twice, ★ skip next Picot, dc in next 2 dc, ch 1, dc in next 2 dc, ch 1, (skip next Picot, dc in next dc, ch 1) twice; repeat from ★ across to last Picot, skip last Picot, dc in last 3 dc.

LADDER ST

Multiple of 7 + 5 chs.

Row 1 (Right side)**:** Sc in second ch from hook, skip next 2 chs, 3 dc in next ch, ★ ch 3, skip next 3 chs, sc in next ch, skip next 2 chs, 3 dc in next ch; repeat from ★ across.

Row 2: Ch 1, turn; sc in first dc, skip next 2 dc, 3 dc in next sc, ★ ch 3, sc in next dc, skip next 2 dc, 3 dc in next sc; repeat from ★ across.

Repeat Row 2 for pattern.

POST RIDGES

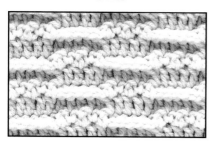

Multiple of 10 + 7 chs.

Row 1 (Right side)**:** Dc in fourth ch from hook **(3 skipped chs count as first dc)** and in each ch across.

To work FPsc, insert hook from **front** to **back** around post of st indicated *(Fig. b)*, YO and pull up a loop, YO and draw through both loops on hook.

Fig. b

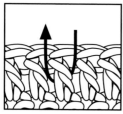

Row 2: Ch 1, turn; work FPsc around first 5 dc, ★ dc in next dc, (sc in next dc, dc in next dc) twice, work FPsc around next 5 dc; repeat from ★ across.

Row 3: Ch 3 **(counts as first dc, now and throughout)**, turn; dc in next FPsc and in each st across.

Row 4: Ch 1, turn; sc in first 2 dc, dc in next dc, sc in next dc, dc in next dc, work FPsc around next 5 dc, dc in next dc, ★ (sc in next dc, dc in next dc) twice, work FPsc around next 5 dc, dc in next dc; repeat from ★ across to last 4 dc, sc in next dc, dc in next dc, sc in last 2 dc.

Row 5: Ch 3, turn; dc in next sc and in each st across.

Repeat Rows 2-5 for pattern.

SC RIDGES

Multiple of 2 chs.

Row 1 (Right side)**:** Sc in second ch from hook, ★ ch 1, skip next ch, sc in next ch; repeat from ★ across.

Row 2: Ch 1, turn; working in Back Loops Only *(Fig. 1, page 31)*, sc in first sc, (ch 1, sc in next sc) across.

Repeat Row 2 for pattern.

DANCING CLUSTERS

Multiple of 4 + 3 chs.

Row 1: Dc in fourth ch from hook **(3 skipped chs count as first dc)** and in next 2 chs, ch 2, ★ skip next ch, dc in next 3 chs, ch 2; repeat from ★ across to last 5 chs, skip next ch, dc in last 4 chs.

To work Cluster (uses one dc), ★ YO, insert hook in dc indicated, YO and pull up a loop, YO and draw through 2 loops on hook; repeat from ★ 2 times **more**, YO and draw through all 4 loops on hook.

Row 2 (Right side)**:** Ch 3 **(counts as first dc, now and throughout)**, turn; skip next dc, work (Cluster, ch 3, Cluster) in next dc, ★ skip next 2 dc, work (Cluster, ch 3, Cluster) in next dc; repeat from ★ across to last 2 dc, skip next dc, dc in last dc.

Row 3: Ch 3, turn; 3 dc in next ch-3 sp, (ch 2, 3 dc in next ch-3 sp) across to last 2 sts, skip next Cluster, dc in last dc.

Row 4: Ch 3, turn; skip next dc, work (Cluster, ch 3, Cluster) in next dc, ★ skip next 2 dc, work (Cluster, ch 3, Cluster) in next dc; repeat from ★ across to last 2 dc, skip next dc, dc in last dc.

Repeat Rows 3 and 4 for pattern.

SC CROSS ST

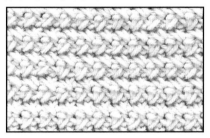

Multiple of 2 chs.

Row 1 (Wrong side)**:** Sc in second ch from hook and in each ch across.

Row 2: Ch 1, turn; sc in first sc, ★ skip next sc, sc in next sc, working **loosely** around sc just made **(Fig. 3, page 32)**, sc in skipped sc; repeat from ★ across.

Repeat Row 2 for pattern.

MINI SPIDERS

Multiple of 10 + 7 chs.

Row 1 (Right side)**:** Sc in second ch from hook and in next 2 chs, ch 2, skip next 2 chs, dc in next ch, ★ ch 2, skip next 2 chs, sc in next 5 chs, ch 2, skip next 2 chs, dc in next ch; repeat from ★ across.

Row 2: Ch 1, turn; sc in first dc and in next ch-2 sp, ch 2, ★ skip next sc, sc in next 3 sc, ch 2, sc in next ch-2 sp, sc in next dc and in next ch-2 sp, ch 2; repeat from ★ across to last 3 sc, skip next sc, sc in last 2 sc.

Row 3: Ch 5 **(counts as first dc plus ch 2)**, turn; sc in next ch-2 sp, ★ sc in next 3 sc and in next ch-2 sp, ch 2, skip next sc, dc in next sc, ch 2, sc in next ch-2 sp; repeat from ★ across to last 2 sc, sc in last 2 sc.

Row 4: Ch 1, turn; sc in first 2 sc, ch 2, sc in next ch-2 sp, ★ sc in next dc and in next ch-2 sp, ch 2, skip next sc, sc in next 3 sc, ch 2, sc in next ch-2 sp; repeat from ★ across to last dc, sc in last dc.

Row 5: Ch 1, turn; sc in first 2 sc and in next ch-2 sp, ch 2, skip next sc, dc in next sc, ★ ch 2, sc in next ch-2 sp, sc in next 3 sc and in next ch-2 sp, ch 2, skip next sc, dc in next sc; repeat from ★ across.

Repeat Rows 2-5 for pattern.

DC TEXTURE

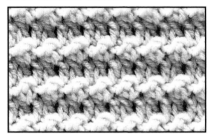

Multiple of 2 + 1 chs.

Row 1 (Right side)**:** Dc in fourth ch from hook **(3 skipped chs count as first dc)** and in each ch across.

Row 2: Turn; slip st in first dc, (dc in next dc, slip st in next dc) across.

Row 3: Ch 3 **(counts as first dc)**, turn; dc in next dc and in each slip st and dc across.

Repeat Rows 2 and 3 for pattern.

CLUSTER STRIPES

Multiple of 3 chs.
Row 1 (Right side)**:** Dc in fourth ch from hook **(3 skipped chs count as first dc)** and in each ch across.
Row 2: Ch 2 **(counts as first hdc, now and throughout)**, turn; hdc in next dc and in each dc across.
To work Cluster (uses one st), ch 3, ★ YO, insert hook in st indicated, YO and pull up a loop, YO and draw through 2 loops on hook; repeat from ★ once **more**, YO and draw through all 3 loops on hook.
To work decrease (uses next 3 hdc), ★ YO, insert hook in **next** hdc, YO and pull up a loop, YO and draw through 2 loops on hook; repeat from ★ 2 times **more**, YO and draw through all 4 loops on hook.
To work ending decrease (uses last 2 hdc), ★ YO, insert hook in **next** hdc, YO and pull up a loop, YO and draw through 2 loops on hook; repeat from ★ once **more**, YO and draw through all 3 loops on hook.

Row 3: Ch 3 **(counts as first dc, now and throughout)**, turn; dc in same st, work Cluster in top of dc just made, skip next hdc, (decrease, work Cluster in top of decrease just made) across to last 2 hdc, work ending decrease.
Row 4: Ch 3, turn; dc in same st, (skip next Cluster, 3 dc in next decrease) across to last Cluster, skip last Cluster and next dc, 2 dc in last dc.
Row 5: Ch 3, turn; dc in next dc and in each dc across.
Row 6: Ch 2, turn; hdc in next dc and in each dc across.
Repeat Rows 3-6 for pattern.

DIAGONAL CLUSTERS

Multiple of 8 + 2 chs.
Row 1 (Right side)**:** Sc in second ch from hook, ★ ch 1, skip next ch, sc in next ch; repeat from ★ across.
Note: Mark Row 1 as **right** side.
To work Cluster Loop, ch 5, ★ YO, insert hook in second ch from hook, YO and pull up a loop, YO and draw through 2 loops on hook; repeat from ★ once **more**, YO and draw through all 3 loops on hook.

Row 2: Ch 1, turn; sc in first sc, ch 1, sc in next sc, work Cluster Loop, skip next sc, sc in next sc, ★ (ch 1, sc in next sc) twice, work Cluster Loop, skip next sc, sc in next sc; repeat from ★ across to last sc, ch 1, sc in last sc.

Push Cluster Loops to **right** side.

Row 3: Ch 1, turn; sc in first sc, ch 1, sc in next sc, ch 3, skip next Cluster Loop, sc in next sc, ★ (ch 1, sc in next sc) twice, ch 3, skip next Cluster Loop, sc in next sc; repeat from ★ across to last sc, ch 1, sc in last sc.

Row 4: Ch 1, turn; sc in first sc, ch 1, sc in next sc, ch 1, working **behind** next ch-3 *(Fig. 3, page 32)*, sc around ch of Cluster Loop one row **below**, work Cluster Loop, ★ skip next sc, (sc in next sc, ch 1) twice, working **behind** next ch-3, sc around ch of Cluster Loop one row **below**, work Cluster Loop; repeat from ★ across to last 2 sc, skip next sc, sc in last sc.

Row 5: Ch 1, turn; sc in first sc, ★ ch 3, skip next Cluster Loop, sc in next sc, (ch 1, sc in next sc) twice; repeat from ★ across.

Row 6: Ch 1, turn; sc in first sc, ch 1, (sc in next sc, ch 1) twice, working **behind** next ch-3, sc around ch of Cluster Loop one row **below**, ★ work Cluster Loop, skip next sc, (sc in next sc, ch 1) twice, working **behind** next ch-3, sc around ch of Cluster Loop one row **below**; repeat from ★ across to last sc, ch 1, sc in last sc.

Row 7: Ch 1, turn; sc in first sc, (ch 1, sc in next sc) 3 times, ch 3, skip next Cluster Loop, sc in next sc, ★ (ch 1, sc in next sc) twice, ch 3, skip next Cluster Loop, sc in next sc; repeat from ★ across to last 3 sc, (ch 1, sc in next sc) 3 times.

Row 8: Ch 1, turn; sc in first sc, work Cluster Loop, skip next sc, (sc in next sc, ch 1) twice, ★ working **behind** next ch-3, sc around ch of Cluster Loop one row **below**, work Cluster Loop, skip next sc, (sc in next sc, ch 1) twice; repeat from ★ across to last sc, sc in last sc.

Row 9: Ch 1, turn; sc in first sc, ★ (ch 1, sc in next sc) twice, ch 3, skip next Cluster Loop, sc in next sc; repeat from ★ across.

Row 10: Ch 1, turn; sc in first sc, ch 1, working **behind** next ch-3, sc around ch of Cluster Loop one row **below**, work Cluster Loop, ★ skip next sc, (sc in next sc, ch 1) twice, working **behind** next ch-3, sc around ch of Cluster Loop one row **below**, work Cluster Loop; repeat from ★ across to last 3 sc, skip next sc, sc in next sc, ch 1, sc in last sc.

Repeat Rows 3-10 for pattern.

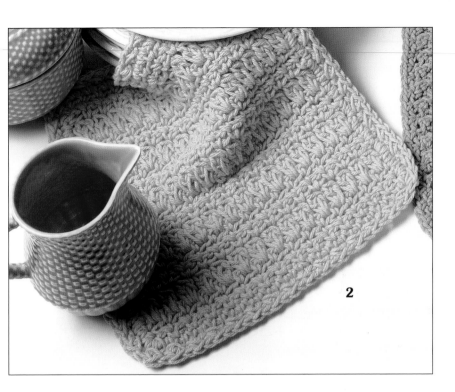

PROJECTS

1. SC RIDGES DISHCLOTH

Shown on page 14.

Finished Size:
8" x 9"

MATERIALS
100% Cotton Worsted Weight Yarn:
$1^3/4$ ounces,
(50 grams, 85 yards)
Crochet hook, size I (5.50 mm)

GAUGE: In pattern,
(sc, ch 1) 10 times and 14 rows = 4"

We used Sc Ridges, page 9, for our Dishcloth.

BODY
Ch 40.

Row 1 (Right side)**:** Working in back ridge of chs *(Fig. 6c, page 33)*, sc in second ch from hook, ★ ch 1, skip next ch, sc in next ch; repeat from ★ across: 20 sc.

Rows 2-28: Ch 1, turn; working in Back Loops Only *(Fig. 1, page 31)*, sc in first sc, (ch 1, sc in next sc) across; do **not** finish off.

EDGING
Rnd 1: Ch 1, turn; working in Back Loops Only, sc in first sc, ch 1, (sc in next sc, ch 1) across; (sc, ch 1) evenly across end of rows; working in Back Loops Only of beginning ch, sc in first ch, ch 1, ★ skip next ch, sc in next ch, ch 1; repeat from ★ across; (sc, ch 1) evenly across end of rows; join with slip st to first sc.

Rnd 2: Ch 1, do **not** turn; sc in same st, ch 1, (sc in next sc, ch 1) around; join with slip st to first sc, finish off.

Design by
Valesha Marshell Kirksey.

2. CLUSTER ROWS DISHCLOTH

Shown on page 14.

Finished Size:
9" x 9½"

MATERIALS
100% Cotton Worsted Weight Yarn:
1¾ ounces,
(50 grams, 85 yards)
Crochet hook, size F (3.75 mm)

GAUGE: In pattern,
(sc, ch 1) 8 times = 4¼";
11 rows = 4"

We used Cluster Rows, page 7, for our Dishcloth.

BODY
Ch 32.

Row 1 (Wrong side)**:** Sc in second ch from hook, ★ ch 1, skip next ch, sc in next ch; repeat from ★ across: 16 sc and 15 ch-1 sps.

Rows 2 and 3: Ch 1, turn; sc in first sc, (ch 1, sc in next sc) across.

To work Cluster (uses one ch-1 sp), ★ YO, insert hook in sp indicated, YO and pull up a loop, YO and draw through 2 loops on hook; repeat from ★ once **more**, YO and draw through all 3 loops on hook.

Row 4: Ch 4 **(counts as first dc plus ch 1)**, turn; (work Cluster in next ch-1 sp, ch 1) across, dc in last sc: 15 Clusters.

Row 5: Ch 1, turn; sc in first dc, ch 1, skip next ch-1 sp, (sc in next ch-1 sp, ch 1) across to last ch-1 sp, skip last ch-1 sp, sc in last dc: 16 sc and 15 ch-1 sps.

Rows 6 and 7: Ch 1, turn; sc in first sc, (ch 1, sc in next sc) across.

Rows 8-23: Repeat Rows 4-7, 4 times; do **not** finish off.

EDGING
Rnd 1: Ch 1, turn; sc evenly around entire piece working an even number of sc and working 3 sc in each corner; join with slip st to first sc.

Rnd 2: Ch 1, do **not** turn; sc in next sc, working **loosely** around sc just made *(Fig. 3, page 32)*, sc in same st as joining, ★ skip next sc, sc in next sc, working **loosely** around sc just made, sc in skipped sc; repeat from ★ around; join with slip st to first sc, finish off.

Design by Valesha Marshell Kirksey.

3. CLASSIC HALF CIRCLE RUG

Shown on page 18.

Finished Size:
19" x 40"

MATERIALS
Worsted Weight Yarn:
Navy - 5 ounces,
(140 grams, 345 yards)
Blue - 4 ounces,
(110 grams, 275 yards)
Ecru - 3 ounces,
(90 grams, 205 yards)
Lt Blue - 1¹/₄ ounces,
(35 grams, 85 yards)
Crochet hook, size Q (15.00 mm)

Note: Rug is worked holding four strands of yarn together throughout.

GAUGE: Rnds 1 and 2 = 3¹/₄" x 8"

We used V-St Pattern, page 4, for our Rug.

With Lt Blue, ch 6.

Row 1 (Right side)**:** 2 Dc in fourth ch from hook, dc in next ch, 3 dc in last ch: 7 sts.

Note: Mark Row 1 as **right** side.

Row 2: Ch 3 **(counts as first dc, now and throughout),** turn; dc in same st, 2 dc in each of next 2 dc, dc in next dc, 2 dc in each of last 3 sts: 13 dc.

Row 3: Ch 3, turn; dc in same st and in next dc, 2 dc in next dc, dc in next dc, 2 dc in next dc, dc in next 3 dc, 2 dc in next dc, (dc in next dc, 2 dc in next dc) twice: 19 dc.

Row 4: Ch 3, turn; dc in same st and in next 2 dc, 2 dc in next dc, dc in next 2 dc, 2 dc in next dc, dc in next 5 dc, 2 dc in next dc, (dc in next 2 dc, 2 dc in next dc) twice; finish off: 25 dc.

To work V-St, (dc, ch 1, dc) in next dc.

To Join With Dc, begin with a slip knot on hook, YO, holding loop on hook, insert hook in st indicated, YO and pull up a loop, (YO and draw through 2 loops on hook) twice.

Row 5: With **right** side facing, join Ecru with dc in first dc; (skip next dc, work V-St) across to last 2 dc, skip next dc, dc in last dc; finish off: 11 V-Sts.

Row 6: With **right** side facing, join Blue with dc in first dc; dc in same st, 2 dc in next ch-1 sp, (skip next dc, dc in next dc, 2 dc in next ch-1 sp) across to last 2 dc, skip next dc, 2 dc in last dc: 36 dc.

Row 7: Ch 3, turn; dc in same st and in next 6 dc, 2 dc in next dc, (dc in next 6 dc, 2 dc in next dc) across: 42 dc.

Row 8: Ch 3, turn; dc in same st and in next 6 dc, 2 dc in next dc, (dc in next 6 dc, 2 dc in next dc) 4 times, dc in next 5 dc, 2 dc in last dc: 49 dc.

Row 9: Ch 3, turn; dc in same st and in next 8 dc, 2 dc in next dc, dc in next 8 dc, 2 dc in next dc, dc in next 11 dc, 2 dc in next dc, (dc in next 8 dc, 2 dc in next dc) twice; finish off: 55 dc.

Row 10: With **right** side facing, join Ecru with dc in first dc; (skip next dc, work V-St, skip next 2 dc, work V-St) 4 times, (skip next dc, work V-St) 7 times, skip next 2 dc, work V-St, (skip next dc, work V-St, skip next 2 dc, work V-St) 3 times, skip next dc, dc in last dc; finish off: 22 V-Sts.

Row 11: With **right** side facing, join Navy with dc in first dc; 2 dc in next ch-1 sp, (skip next dc, dc in next dc, 2 dc in next ch-1 sp) across to last 2 dc, skip next dc, dc in last dc: 67 dc.

Row 12: Ch 3, turn; (dc in next 8 dc, 2 dc in next dc) twice, (dc in next 9 dc, 2 dc in next dc) 3 times, dc in next 8 dc, 2 dc in next dc, dc in last 9 dc: 73 dc.

Row 13: Ch 3, turn; dc in next 7 dc, 2 dc in next dc, dc in next 9 dc, 2 dc in next dc, dc in next 10 dc, 2 dc in next dc, dc in next 13 dc, 2 dc in next dc, dc in next 10 dc, 2 dc in next dc, dc in next 9 dc, 2 dc in next dc, dc in last 8 dc; finish off: 79 dc.

To Join With Sc, begin with a slip knot on hook. Insert hook in dc indicated, YO and pull up a loop, YO and draw through both loops on hook.

Row 14: With **right** side facing, join Ecru with sc in first dc; (ch 3, skip next dc, sc in next dc) across; finish off.

Design by Maggie Weldon.

5

6

4. SHELLS & LACE BABY WRAP

Shown on page 17.

Finished Size:
34" x 42"

MATERIALS
Sport Weight Yarn:
14 ounces,
(400 grams, 1,400 yards)
Crochet hook, size H (5.00 mm)
or size needed for gauge

GAUGE: In pattern,
(sc, Shell) 4 times and Rows
1-13 = 6"

We used Shells & Lace, page 4, for our Baby Afghan.

AFGHAN BODY
Ch 98.

To work Shell, 5 dc in st or sp indicated.

Row 1 (Right side)**:** Sc in second ch from hook, ★ skip next 2 chs, work Shell in next ch, skip next 2 chs, sc in next ch; repeat from ★ across: 16 Shells and 17 sc.

Row 2: Ch 5 **(counts as first dc plus ch 2, now and throughout)**, turn; sc in center dc of next Shell, ch 2, dc in next sc, ★ ch 2, sc in center dc of next Shell, ch 2, dc in next sc; repeat from ★ across: 33 sts and 32 ch-2 sps.

Row 3: Ch 6 **(counts as first dc plus ch 3)**, turn; sc in next sc, ch 3, dc in next dc, ★ ch 3, sc in next sc, ch 3, dc in next dc; repeat from ★ across.

Row 4: Ch 1, turn; sc in first dc, ★ ch 2, dc in next sc, ch 2, sc in next dc; repeat from ★ across.

Row 5: Ch 1, turn; sc in first sc, (work Shell in next dc, sc in next sc) across: 16 Shells and 17 sc.

Rows 6-74: Repeat Rows 2-5, 17 times; then repeat Row 2 once **more**; do **not** finish off.

BORDER

Rnd 1: Ch 1, turn; sc in first dc, (2 sc in next ch-2 sp, sc in next sc, 2 sc in next ch-2 sp, sc in next dc) across, place marker around last sc made for st placement; working in end of rows, 3 sc in first row, sc in next 2 rows, (2 sc in each of next 2 rows, sc in next 2 rows) across to last 3 rows, 2 sc in each of last 3 rows; working in free loops and in sps across beginning ch *(Fig. 2, page 32)*, sc in first ch, place marker around sc just made for st placement, (2 sc in next sp, sc in ch at base of next Shell, 2 sc in next sp, sc in ch at base of next sc) across, place marker around last sc made for st placement; working in end of rows, 2 sc in each of first 3 rows, sc in next 2 rows, (2 sc in each of next 2 rows, sc in next 2 rows) across to last row, 3 sc in last row; join with slip st to first sc: 420 sc.

Rnd 2: Ch 3 **(counts as first dc, now and throughout)**, do **not** turn; 2 dc in same st, ★ dc in each sc across to next marked sc, work Shell in marked sc; repeat from ★ 2 times **more**, dc in each sc across, 2 dc in same st as first dc; join with slip st to first dc: 436 dc.

Rnd 3: Ch 1, sc in same st, skip next dc, work Shell in next dc, (skip next 2 dc, sc in next dc, skip next 2 dc, work Shell in next dc) across working last Shell in first dc of next corner Shell, skip next dc, ★ sc in next dc (center dc of corner Shell), skip next dc, work Shell in next dc, (skip next 2 dc, sc in next dc, skip next 2 dc, work Shell in next dc) across working last Shell in first dc of next corner Shell, skip next dc; repeat from ★ 2 times **more**; join with slip st to first sc: 74 Shells.

Rnd 4: Ch 5, dc in same st, ch 2, sc in center dc of next Shell, ch 2, (dc in next sc, ch 2, sc in center dc of next Shell, ch 2) across to next corner sc, ★ (dc, ch 2) 3 times in corner sc, sc in center dc of next Shell, ch 2, (dc in next sc, ch 2, sc in center dc of next Shell, ch 2) across to next corner sc; repeat from ★ 2 times **more**, dc in same st as first dc, ch 2; join with slip st to first dc: 156 sts and 156 ch-2 sps.

Rnd 5: Ch 1, 2 sc in same st, ★ † 3 sc in next ch-2 sp, 2 sc in next dc and in next ch-2 sp, (sc in next sc, 2 sc in next ch-2 sp, sc in next dc, 2 sc in next ch-2 sp) across to center dc of next corner 3-dc group †, 3 sc in center dc; repeat from ★ 2 times **more**, then repeat from † to † once, sc in same st as first sc; join with slip st to first sc: 484 sc.

Rnd 6: Ch 3, dc in same st and in each sc across to center sc of next corner 3-sc group, ★ 3 dc in center sc, dc in each sc across to center sc of next corner 3-sc group; repeat from ★ 2 times **more**, dc in same st as first dc; join with slip st to first dc: 492 dc.

Rnd 7: Ch 1, (sc in same st, ch 5) twice, skip next 2 dc, (sc in next dc, ch 5, skip next 2 dc) across to center dc of next corner 3-dc group, ★ (sc, ch 5) twice in center dc, skip next 2 dc, (sc in next dc, ch 5, skip next 2 dc) across to center dc of next corner 3-dc group; repeat from ★ 2 times **more**; join with slip st to first sc: 168 ch-5 sps.

Rnd 8: Slip st in first ch-5 sp, ch 3, 8 dc in same sp, sc in next ch-5 sp, ch 3, sc in next ch-5 sp, (work Shell in next ch-5 sp, sc in next ch-5 sp, ch 3, sc in next ch-5 sp) across to next corner ch-5 sp, ★ 9 dc in corner ch-5 sp, sc in next ch-5 sp, ch 3, sc in next ch-5 sp, (work Shell in next ch-5 sp, sc in next ch-5 sp, ch 3, sc in next ch-5 sp) across to next corner ch-5 sp; repeat from ★ 2 times **more**; join with slip st to first dc: 52 Shells, 4 9-dc groups, and 56 ch-3 sps.

Rnd 9: Slip st in next 2 dc, ch 5, dc in same st, ch 2, skip next dc, (dc, ch 2) 5 times in next dc, skip next dc, (dc, ch 2, dc) in next dc, ch 1, sc in next ch-3 sp, ch 1, † dc in center dc of next Shell, (ch 2, dc in same st) 4 times, ch 1, sc in next ch-3 sp, ch 1 †; repeat from † to † across to next corner 9-dc group, skip first 2 dc of corner 9-dc group, ★ (dc, ch 2) twice in next dc, skip next dc, (dc, ch 2) 5 times in next dc, skip next dc, (dc, ch 2, dc) in next dc, ch 1, sc in next ch-3 sp, ch 1, repeat from † to † across to next corner 9-dc group, skip first 2 dc of corner 9-dc group; repeat from ★ 2 times **more**; join with slip st to first dc.

Rnd 10: Ch 1, sc in same st, † (ch 3, sc in next dc) 8 times, skip next 2 ch-1 sps, sc in next dc, [(ch 3, sc in next dc) 4 times, skip next 2 ch-1 sps, sc in next dc] 12 times, (ch 3, sc in next dc) 8 times, skip next 2 ch-1 sps †, sc in next dc, [(ch 3, sc in next dc) 4 times, skip next 2 ch-1 sps, sc in next dc] 14 times, repeat from † to † once, [sc in next dc, (ch 3, sc in next dc) 4 times, skip next 2 ch-1 sps] across; join with slip st to first sc, finish off.

Design by Terry Kimbrough.

5. VINTAGE AFGHAN

Shown on page 21.

Finished Size:
42" x 57"

MATERIALS
Worsted Weight Yarn:
47 ounces,
(1,330 grams, 2,270 yards)
Crochet hook, size I (5.50 mm)
or size needed for gauge

GAUGE: In pattern,
12 sts and Rows 1-10 = 4"

We used Extended tr, page 3, for our Afghan.

Note: Each row is worked across length of Afghan.

AFGHAN
Ch 173.

Row 1: Dc in back ridge of fourth ch from hook *(Fig. 6c, page 33)* and each ch across **(3 skipped chs count as first dc)**: 171 dc.

Row 2 (Right side)**:** Ch 1, turn; sc in each dc across.

Note: Mark Row 2 as **right** side.

Row 3: Ch 3 **(counts as first dc, now and throughout)**, turn; dc in next sc and in each sc across.

Row 4: Ch 1, turn; sc in each dc across.

To work Extended Treble Crochet (abbreviated ex tr), YO twice, insert hook in next st, YO and pull up a loop (4 loops on hook), (YO and draw through one loop on hook, YO and draw through 2 loops on hook) 3 times. Push ex tr to **right** side.

Row 5: Ch 1, turn; sc in first sc, (work ex tr, sc in next sc) across: 85 ex tr and 86 sc.

Row 6: Ch 3, turn; dc in next st and in each st across: 171 dc.

Rows 7 and 8: Ch 1, turn; sc in each st across.

Row 9: Ch 1, turn; sc in first 7 sc, work ex tr, (sc in next 11 sc, work ex tr) across to last 7 sc, sc in last 7 sc: 14 ex tr and 157 sc.

Row 10: Ch 3, turn; dc in next st and in each st across: 171 dc.

Row 11: Ch 1, turn; sc in first 5 dc, work ex tr, (sc in next dc, work ex tr) twice, ★ sc in next 7 dc, work ex tr, (sc in next dc, work ex tr) twice; repeat from ★ across to last 5 dc, sc in last 5 dc: 42 ex tr and 129 sc.

Row 12: Ch 3, turn; dc in next st and in each st across: 171 dc.

Row 13: Ch 1, turn; sc in first 7 dc, work ex tr, (sc in next 11 dc, work ex tr) across to last 7 dc, sc in last 7 dc: 14 ex tr and 157 sc.

Rows 14 and 15: Ch 1, turn; sc in each st across: 171 sc.

Row 16: Ch 3, turn; dc in next sc and in each sc across.

Row 17: Ch 1, turn; sc in first dc, (work ex tr, sc in next dc) across: 85 ex tr and 86 sc.

Row 18: Ch 1, turn; sc in each st across: 171 sc.

Row 19: Ch 3, turn; dc in next sc and in each sc across.

Rows 20-26: Repeat Rows 18 and 19, 3 times; then repeat Row 18 once **more**.

Rows 27-109: Repeat Rows 5-26, 3 times; then repeat Rows 5-21 once **more**; at end of Row 109, finish off.

Holding 7 strands of yarn together, each 16" long, add fringe evenly spaced across short edges of Afghan **(Figs. 4a & b, page 32)**.

Design by Mary Lamb Becker.

---

6. DIAGONAL CLUSTERS PILLOW

Shown on page 22.

Finished Size:
16" square

MATERIALS
Worsted Weight Yarn:
9 ounces,
(260 grams, 510 yards)
Crochet hooks, sizes H (5.00 mm) and I (5.50 mm) **or** sizes needed for gauge
Pillow form - 16" square
Fabric - $1/2$ yard for lining (optional)

GAUGE: With larger size hook, in pattern,
15 sts and 15 rows = 4"

We used Diagonal Clusters, page 12, for our Pillow.

PILLOW COVER
(Make 2)
With larger size hook, ch 58.
Row 1 (Right side)**:** Sc in second ch from hook, ★ ch 1, skip next ch, sc in next ch; repeat from ★ across: 29 sc and 28 sps.

Note: Mark Row 1 as **right** side.

To work Cluster Loop, ch 5, ★ YO, insert hook in second ch from hook, YO and pull up a loop, YO and draw through 2 loops on hook; repeat from ★ once **more**, YO and draw through all 3 loops on hook.

Row 2: Ch 1, turn; sc in first sc, ch 1, sc in next sc, work Cluster Loop, skip next sc, sc in next sc, ★ (ch 1, sc in next sc) twice, work Cluster Loop, skip next sc, sc in next sc; repeat from ★ across to last sc, ch 1, sc in last sc: 22 sc and 7 Cluster Loops.

Push Cluster Loops to **right** side.

Row 3: Ch 1, turn; sc in first sc, ch 1, sc in next sc, ch 3, skip next Cluster Loop, sc in next sc, ★ (ch 1, sc in next sc) twice, ch 3, skip next Cluster Loop, sc in next sc; repeat from ★ across to last sc, ch 1, sc in last sc.

Row 4: Ch 1, turn; sc in first sc, ch 1, sc in next sc, ch 1, working **behind** next ch-3 *(Fig. 3, page 32)*, sc around ch of Cluster Loop one row **below**, work Cluster Loop, ★ skip next sc, (sc in next sc, ch 1) twice, working **behind** next ch-3, sc around ch of Cluster Loop one row **below**, work Cluster Loop; repeat from ★ across to last 2 sc, skip next sc, sc in last sc.

Row 5: Ch 1, turn; sc in first sc, ★ ch 3, skip next Cluster Loop, sc in next sc, (ch 1, sc in next sc) twice; repeat from ★ across.

Row 6: Ch 1, turn; sc in first sc, ch 1, (sc in next sc, ch 1) twice, working **behind** next ch-3, sc around ch of Cluster Loop one row **below**, ★ work Cluster Loop, skip next sc, (sc in next sc, ch 1) twice, working **behind** next ch-3, sc around ch of Cluster Loop one row **below**; repeat from ★ across to last sc, ch 1, sc in last sc: 23 sc and 6 Cluster Loops.

Row 7: Ch 1, turn; sc in first sc, (ch 1, sc in next sc) 3 times, ch 3, skip next Cluster Loop, sc in next sc, ★ (ch 1, sc in next sc) twice, ch 3, skip next Cluster Loop, sc in next sc; repeat from ★ across to last 3 sc, (ch 1, sc in next sc) 3 times.

Row 8: Ch 1, turn; sc in first sc, work Cluster Loop, skip next sc, (sc in next sc, ch 1) twice, ★ working **behind** next ch-3, sc around ch of Cluster Loop one row **below**, work Cluster Loop, skip next sc, (sc in next sc, ch 1) twice; repeat from ★ across to last sc, sc in last sc: 22 sc and 7 Cluster Loops.

Row 9: Ch 1, turn; sc in first sc, ★ (ch 1, sc in next sc) twice, ch 3, skip next Cluster Loop, sc in next sc; repeat from ★ across.

Row 10: Ch 1, turn; sc in first sc, ch 1, working **behind** next ch-3, sc around ch of Cluster Loop one row **below**, work Cluster Loop, ★ skip next sc, (sc in next sc, ch 1) twice, working **behind** next ch-3, sc around ch of Cluster Loop one row **below**, work Cluster Loop; repeat from ★ across to last 3 sc, skip next sc, sc in next sc, ch 1, sc in last sc.

Rows 11-55: Repeat Rows 3-10, 5 times; then repeat Rows 3-7 once **more**.

Row 56: Ch 1, turn; sc in first sc, ★ (ch 1, sc in next sc) 3 times, ch 1, working **behind** next ch-3, sc around ch of Cluster Loop one row **below**; repeat from ★ across to last 4 sc, (ch 1, sc in next sc) 4 times: 29 sc and 28 sps.

Row 57: Ch 1, turn; sc in first sc, (ch 1, sc in next sc) across; do **not** finish off.

BORDER

Change to smaller size hook.

Do **not** turn; working in one loop of each st across end of rows, slip st in first row, place marker around slip st just made for joining, slip st in each row across, ch 1, place marker around ch just made to mark corner; working in free loops of beginning ch **(Fig. 2, page 32)** and in skipped chs, slip st in each ch across, ch 1, place marker around ch just made to mark corner; working in one loop of each st across end of rows, slip st in first row and in each row across, ch 1, place marker around ch just made to mark corner; slip st in Front Loop Only **(Fig. 1, page 31)** of each st across Row 57, ch 1, place marker around ch just made to mark corner; join with slip st to marked slip st, remove marker from slip st, finish off.

ASSEMBLY

Cover pillow form with fabric, if desired.

Place **wrong** sides of Pillow Covers together, matching stitches and rows. With smaller size hook and working through **both** loops of **both** pieces, join yarn with slip st in any corner; slip st in each st around three sides, insert pillow form and slip st across last side; join with slip st to first st, finish off.

Design by Anne Halliday.

GENERAL INSTRUCTIONS

ABBREVIATIONS

ch(s)	chain(s)
dc	double crochet(s)
ex tr	extended treble crochet(s)
FPsc	Front Post single crochet(s)
hdc	half double crochet(s)
LSC	Long Single Crochet(s)
mm	millimeters
Rnd(s)	Round(s)
sc	single crochet(s)
sp(s)	space(s)
st(s)	stitch(es)
YO	yarn over

★ — work instructions following ★ as many **more** times as indicated in addition to the first time.

† to † — work all instructions from first † to second † **as many** times as specified.

( ) or [ ] — work enclosed instructions **as many** times as specified by the number immediately following **or** work all enclosed instructions in the stitch or space indicated **or** contains explanatory remarks.

colon (:) — the number(s) given after a colon at the end of a row or round denote(s) the number of stitches or spaces you should have on that row or round.

MULTIPLES

The multiple for each pattern stitch is listed below the ID Photo. The multiple indicates the number of chains required to form one complete pattern of the design.

Different pattern stitches produce a different number of stitches and/or rows per inch with the same yarn and the same size hook. Therefore, patterns which share the same multiple will not necessarily be interchangeable, because each may produce a different gauge.

GAUGE

Gauge refers to the number of stitches and rows in a given area. The size of a stitch will vary depending on the yarn, the size of your hook, and the way you control the yarn. In the Pattern Stitch section, there is no gauge or hook size specified because each pattern can be worked in your choice of yarn to vary the size and appearance of the design.

In the Project section, correct gauge is essential for proper size or fit. Hook sizes given in instructions are merely guides and should never be used without first making a sample swatch approximately 4" square in the stitch, yarn, and hook specified. Then measure it, counting your stitches and rows carefully. If your swatch is larger or smaller than specified, **make another, changing hook size to get the correct gauge**. Keep trying until you find the size hook that will give you the specified gauge. Once proper gauge is obtained, measure the width of the piece approximately every 3" to be sure gauge remains consistent.

YARN

Before choosing the yarn and hooks for your project, you may want to experiment with a variety of weights until you achieve the appearance and texture that you desire. Yarn weight (type or size) is divided into six basic categories:

Fingering: Fine weight yarns that make great socks and beautiful baby clothes.

Sport: Most often used for light-weight sweaters, baby clothes, and baby afghans.

Double Knit: Most often used for sweaters and afghans.

Worsted: Makes great sweaters, vests, and afghans.

Heavy Worsted: Most often used for heavy sweaters and afghans.

Bulky: Generally used to make heavy sweaters, jackets, and coats.

BACK OR FRONT LOOP ONLY

Work only in loop(s) indicated by arrow *(Fig. 1)*.

Fig. 1

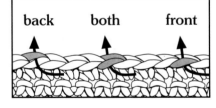

FREE LOOPS OF A CHAIN

When instructed to work in free loops of a chain, work in loop indicated by arrow *(Fig. 2)*.

Fig. 2

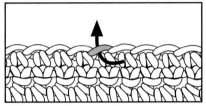

WORKING IN FRONT OF, AROUND, OR BEHIND A STITCH

Work in stitch or space indicated, inserting hook in direction of arrow *(Fig. 3)*.

Fig. 3

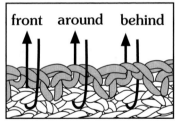

FRINGE

Cut a piece of cardboard 3" wide and half as long as strands specified in individual instructions. Wind the yarn **loosely** and **evenly** around the cardboard lengthwise until the card is filled, then cut across one end; repeat as needed.

Hold together as many strands of yarn as specified in individual instructions; fold in half.

With **wrong** side facing and using a crochet hook, draw the folded end up through a row and pull the loose ends through the folded end *(Fig. 4a)*; draw the knot up **tightly** *(Fig. 4b)*. Repeat, spacing as specified in individual instructions.

Lay flat on a hard surface and trim the ends.

Fig. 4a

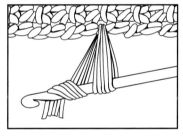

Fig. 4b

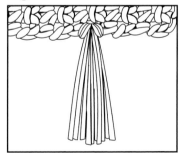

BASIC STITCHES

CHAIN

To work a chain stitch, begin with a slip knot on the hook. Bring the yarn **over** hook from back to front, catching the yarn with the hook and turning the hook slightly toward you to keep the yarn from slipping off. Draw the yarn through the slip knot *(Fig. 5)* **(first chain st made,** *abbreviated ch)*.

Fig. 5

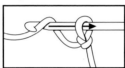

WORKING INTO THE CHAIN

When counting chains, always begin with the first chain from the hook and then count toward the beginning of your foundation chain *(Fig. 6a)*.

Fig. 6a

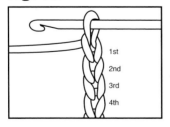

1st
2nd
3rd
4th

Method 1: Insert hook under top two strands of each chain *(Fig. 6b)*.

Fig. 6b

Method 2: Insert hook into back ridge of each chain *(Fig. 6c)*.

Fig. 6c

SLIP STITCH

To work a slip stitch, insert hook in st or sp indicated, YO and draw through st and through loop on hook *(Fig. 7)* **(slip stitch made,** *abbreviated slip st)*.

Fig. 7

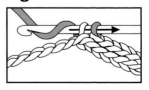